D0674089

So You're a
Grandparent*!*

Mike Haskins & Clive Whichelow

summersdale

SO YOU'RE A GRANDPARENT!

Summersdale Publishers Ltd
46 West Street
Chichester
West Sussex
PO19 1RP
UK

www.summersdale.com

Printed and bound by Imago

ISBN: 1-84024-645-6
ISBN 13: 978-1-84024-645-2

INTRODUCTION

Hello granddad/grandma!

Oh no! There's a name you never thought you'd have!!!

Not when you're still such a lithe desirable sexy young thing (even if you do say so yourself). Not someone still in the prime of life (this is still you, we're talking about by the way), someone who still wears jeans, listens to loud music and, if not in mint condition, is still in reasonably full working order.

Nevertheless your name has now officially been changed.

Hello granddad/grandma!

And it's not just going to be the grandchildren who call you that is it? From now on that's the way their mum and dad are going to refer to you all the time too! It's going to make people think that you're their grandparents as well!

However old you really are and whatever you may actually look like, your new name will conjure up images of grey hair, walking sticks and dreadful soup-stained old cardigans. And to your grandchildren you'll seem as though you're from another century. Come to think of it, you are from another century. Scary or what?

But that's not the worst thing. Oh no! Cast your mind back to when your kids were little. Remember when they kept pleading with you to buy them a puppy, a kitten, a rabbit, any kind of little pet?

'Oh no!' you told them. 'Because I'll tell you exactly what will happen. Pretty soon you'll find you're far too busy and I'll be the one who ends up looking after them each day and cleaning up all the mess.'

Isn't that exactly what has just happened now? Except this time you don't have a receipt to take back to the pet shop for a refund?

Never mind, your grandchildren are absolutely lovely aren't they?

Just look at them!

OK, better fetch some disinfectant and a cleaning cloth quickly and then you can consider how lovely they are.

THE BASIC MYTHS ABOUT BEING A GRANDPARENT

It's all the pleasure and none of the problems of being a parent – no, it's all the pleasure and none of the child benefit payments!

Being with your grandchildren will give you a new lease of life – if they don't cause your premature demise first.

Your grandchildren will regard you as a wonderful, twinkly-eyed old character – more likely your grandchildren will constantly tell you that you smell funny.

THE ADVANTAGES OF BEING A GRANDPARENT

If the kids play up when you're out with them you can tell passers-by it's all the parents' fault.

The kids can act as your spies to keep you informed about what's really going on between their mum and dad.

You can smugly talk about how much harder it was bringing up babies in your day – your kids were too young back then to remember.

You can bribe the kids by offering them all the things their mum and dad say they must definitely never have.

THE DRAWBACKS OF BEING A GRANDPARENT

All the methods you used to discipline your kids are now banned under EU law and international human rights treaties.

Your redundancy pay-off will be severely dented by trips to theme parks.

Half the kids' toys in the attic you wanted to pass on are now deemed politically incorrect.

When you try to help them with their homework you're told, 'We don't do it that way any more.'

ESSENTIAL REQUIREMENTS
FOR BEING A GRANDDAD

The magical ability to produce coins
from behind children's ears

A selection of elderly, yellowing board
games which you insist are more
fun than an afternoon messing
about on the Xbox

A war wound or at least something that could conceivably pass for one e.g. a particularly deep wrinkle

A big bald head shiny enough for the grandchildren to see their reflections in

Physical oddities such as big ears or a hairy nose that can be gleefully pointed out to everyone at family gatherings

ESSENTIAL REQUIREMENTS FOR BEING A GRANDMA

A degree of patience that
passeth all understanding

A variety of fail-safe recipes for
cakes, biscuits, buns, etc.

A giant dressing-up box of bizarre and comical outfits (i.e. your wardrobe)

Photograph albums of the children's parents when they were screaming their heads off over something

An old tin full of buttons that are strangely more fascinating than any toy ever invented

DIFFERENT WAYS YOU WILL BE ASKED: 'ARE YOU AVAILABLE FOR BABYSITTING?'

'The kids keep asking when they can see grandma and granddad again.'

'It must get a bit dull for you sitting in your house night after night...'

'Do you know, the kids absolutely love having you tell them a bedtime story.'

'Trust me, they're all tucked up in bed and fast asleep each night by 6.30 p.m.'

THINGS YOU WILL COME TO KNOW A LOT ABOUT

The lifestyles, thoughts and opinions
of the entire population of the
island of Balamory

All the latest playground insults

The names of all the up-and-coming gangsta rappers

The words (if you can call them words)
to all the latest pop songs (if you
can call them songs)

Details of the goriest horror films
currently available on DVD

DISCIPLINING CHILDREN THE GRANDPARENT WAY

'If you don't behave I will take my teeth out in front of you.'

'If you don't behave, your dinner will be whatever I can find in my kitchen cupboard that's furthest past its use-by date.'

'Don't forget that because I am so old I know a lot of people who have died and if necessary I will contact them and get them to come and haunt you.'

'The law only says *parents* can't smack children you know.'

THINGS YOU'D FORGOTTEN
ABOUT SMALL CHILDREN

The surprising amount they
actually weigh

They view every one of your
possessions as a new toy.

They have no inhibitions about pointing out the most personal and embarrassing of things in the loudest of voices.

They don't enjoy looking round old churches or having a 'nice sit down'.

GRANDPARENT BEHAVIOUR YOU WILL FIND YOURSELF FALLING INTO

Threatening to tell a policeman/Father Christmas/the Tooth Fairy about bad behaviour

Buying boiled sweets because they're the only ones the kids aren't allowed

Recounting details of your childhood
as though it was spent in Dickensian
squalor and poverty

TELLTALE SIGNS THAT YOU'RE A GRANDPARENT

'Baby on board' sticker on your stairlift

Crayon 'artwork' on your fridge door

What looks like the local police station's entire fingerprint collection over your walls and furniture

Misshapen plastic safety covers over your plug sockets covered in teeth marks

PRESENTS YOU WILL BE GIVEN BY YOUR GRANDCHILDREN

A painting of what would appear to be
the oldest person ever to have lived with
your name scrawled across the bottom

Near replicas of heirlooms which have recently met with unfortunate accidents

Various pieces of jewellery made from dried pasta, feathers, seashells, etc.

A clay model of an animal that cannot quite be identified

A box of chocolates which they will immediately insist on unwrapping and helping you to eat

THE GRANDPARENT'S
DAILY SCHEDULE

 7.00 a.m.
Get up.

 7.10 a.m.
Make nice cup of tea.

 7.25 a.m.
Babysitting hotline rings.

7.45 a.m.
Ring on doorbell.

8.00 a.m.
The next few hours pass in something of a blur.

7.00 p.m.-ish
Parents collect kids, apologise for lateness, say they hope the kids haven't been too much trouble!

7.15 p.m.
Five minutes restoring the house to something like order before the next blitzkrieg.

8.00 p.m.
Another nice cup of tea.

8.15 p.m.
Pass out exhausted.

HOW YOUR GRANDCHILDREN
WILL PERCEIVE YOU

As an ultimate authority and source of
wisdom on all matters (apart perhaps
from new technology)

As virtually indestructible

As 'option B' when their parents refuse them something

As a strange wrinkled being with an extremely tidy house

As the only person in the world who can tell *their* mum and dad off

That person who stands there waving with a stupid grin on their face every single time you go past them on the merry-go-round

WHITE LIES TOLD BY GRANDPARENTS

'Granddad/grandma has a very weak heart so it's important for you to be very quiet and well-behaved...'

'I'm not allowed in theme parks at my age.'

'I most certainly do have Father Christmas' mobile phone number.'

'No, we don't have any money. We had to give it all to your parents when you came along.'

THINGS YOU WILL NOW FIND AROUND YOUR HOUSE

Leaflets for all tourist attractions within a 20-mile radius

Various artefacts inscribed with the legend 'To the best granddad/grandma in the world'

A range of toys that came as free gifts with kiddies' burger meals

Half-chewed sweets, biscuits and
sticky things that aren't even
meant to be sticky

Strange wet patches

PHRASES YOU'LL NOW FIND YOURSELF USING

'Five hundred pounds for a pram? We've still got your old one in the attic.'

'If I'd said that to my father he would have knocked me into the middle of next week.'

'They don't know they're born do they?'

And remember, even if you've only got
one grandchild at the moment, call
them 'dear' it'll save remembering
all those names when the rest
of the brood arrives.

PHRASES YOU REALLY SHOULDN'T USE NOW YOU'RE A GRANDPARENT

'Five pounds for a new dummy? We've still got your old one in the attic.'

'Dig my allotment and this entire shiny five-pence piece can be yours.'

'That's not how you draw a tree!'

'Nip down the corner and get me some fags would you?'

THINGS YOUR GRANDCHILDREN WILL TEACH YOU

That you are destroying the planet and personally murdering all the polar bears

How to work your computer,
DVD player and mobile phone

That there are very good reasons why
you are biologically prevented from
having children after a certain age

BARGAINING COUNTERS THAT YOU CAN USE AS A GRANDPARENT

'Of course we wouldn't be able to do all this babysitting if you put us in a home.'

'The kids said next time you bring them round they'll show us how to put some of those old photos of you up on the Internet...'

'If you pay for satellite TV for us the kids can watch cartoons when they come over.'

BAD WAYS GRANDPARENTS CAN ENTERTAIN THE GRANDCHILDREN

Taking out false teeth and gurning

Performing ill-advised
attempts at contortionism

Letting them do exactly what they
say they want to do

BAD WAYS GRANDCHILDREN CAN ENTERTAIN GRANDPARENTS

Making an impromptu piece of modern art involving granny's sofa and a tub of nappy rash cream

Testing out their new teeth on legs (human or furniture)

Hiding and/or sampling granddad
or grandma's various
prescription medicines

Acting out an aerial stunt sequence they
recently saw in a superhero movie

THINGS PEOPLE WILL NOW SAY TO YOU

'You look far too young to be a
grandparent.' (You wish!)

'Oh they'll give you a new lease of life!'
(You poor old codger)

'Nan Nan' or 'Dag Dag' (This is your new long-lost Teletubby name which your grandchildren will call you extremely loudly in public places.)

'They're quite a handful aren't they?'
(This phrase usually prefaces the
speaker making his or her excuses and
leaving you to it.)

'It must really bring back what it was
like when your own children were little.'
(Yes it does and that's why we didn't
have any more of them.)

MAIN EVENTS YOU CAN LOOK FORWARD TO

Seeing them take their
first faltering steps

Hearing them say their first words

Those first little teeth coming through

EVENTS IT'S LESS EASY TO LOOK FORWARD TO

Their first solid foods coming back in slightly less solid form

Them growing up and wanting £100
trainers for Christmas

Hearing them say their first swear words

YOUR NEW SOCIAL CIRCLE

The owner of your local sweet shop

Imaginary friends of your grandchildren

The occasional head louse

GRANDPARENTS' CV

Skills: getting to the end of one's tether
and having to find just a little bit more
tether, seeing the good in children
when no one else can

Education: school of hard knocks,
university of life, night school
of sleep deprivation

Qualifications: Oh! Levels in children's
shocking behaviour, Ah! Levels
in indulgence

WORDS OF WISDOM YOUR GRANDCHILDREN WILL SHARE WITH YOU

'Mummy/daddy says you've lost your marbles. Shall I help you find them?'

'Are your ears and nose getting bigger or are they staying the same size while the rest of your head shrinks?'

'Grandma has lots of lines on her face.'

THINGS YOU REALLY SHOULDN'T BUY FOR YOUR GRANDCHILDREN

Toys that require £10 worth of batteries every three days

Any toy that genuinely fires, shoots, hammers, drills or makes food that they will seriously expect you to sample

Any toy that you will end up having to construct

ADVICE YOU WISH YOU'D BEEN GIVEN

If you have lots of children you will have twice as many grandchildren.

Get all babysitting arrangements in writing.

Don't give them food that can
a) be broken into pieces
b) be smeared or c) stain.

www.summersdale.com